ISABEL, FERDINAND

and Fifteenth-Century Spain

by Kenny Mann

BENCHMARK BOOKS

MARSHALL CAVENDISH
NEW YORK

ACKNOWLEDGMENTS

With thanks to Jarbel Rodriguez, Assistant Professor, San Francisco State University, for his expert reading of the manuscript.

And special thanks to Miriam Greenblatt, who developed the concept for the Rulers and Their Times series.

Benchmark Books
Marshall Cavendish Corporation
99 White Plains Road
Tarrytown, New York 10591-9001
Website: www.marshallcavendish.com

Copyright © 2002 by Marshall Cavendish

Library of Congress Cataloging-in-Publication Data
Mann, Kenny.
Isabel, Ferdinand and fifteenth century Spain / by Kenny Mann.
p. cm.—(Rulers and their times)
Includes bibliographical references and index.
ISBN 0-7614-1030-9 (lib. bdg.)
1. Ferdinand V, King of Spain, 1452–1516—Juvenile literature. 2. Isabella I, Queen of Spain 1451–1504—Juveline literature. [1. Spain—History—Ferdinand and Isabella, 1479–1516—Juvenile literature. 2. Spain—History—Ferdinand and Isabella, 1479–1516. 3. Ferdinand V, King of Spain, 1452–1516. 4. Isabella I, Queen of Spain, 1451–1504. 5. Kings, queens, rulers, etc.] I. Title: Isabel and Ferdinand and 15th Century Spain. II. Series.
DP162.M32   2001   946'.03'0922—dc21   00-041450

Printed in Hong Kong
1 3 5 6 4 2

Photo research by Linda Sykes Picture Research, Hilton Head SC
Cover, 13, 33 (top), 33 (bottom): Dagli Orti/The Art Archive; page 8: Laurie Platt Winfrey Inc.; page 9: Christie's London/Superstock; page 11: British Library/ Bridgeman Art Library; pages 14–15: Town Hall, Malaga, Spain/Bridgeman Art Library; page 17: AKG London; page 19: Musee Bonnat, Bayonee, France/Bridgeman Art Library; page 21: Prado, Madrid/AKG London; page 22: Instituto Municipal de Historia, Barcelona/Bridgeman Art Library; page 27: Kunsthistorisches, Vienna/Art Resource NY; page 30: Academia, Madrid/The Art Archive; pages 36–37: Plaza des Espana, Seville/Annete Godefroid/AKG London; page 38: Pierpont Morgan Library/Art Resource NY; pages 41, 68: The Art Archive; pages 44–45: Prado, Madrid/Giraudon/Art Resource NY; page 47: Palacio Real de Madrid/Bridgeman Art Library; page 51: Private Collection/Bridgeman Art Library; page 52: National Maritime Museum, Greenwich/Werner Forman/Art Resource NY; page 54: Vesailles/Reunion des Musees Nationaux/Art Resource NY; page 56: Scala/Art Resource NY; pages 60–61: Caylus Anticuario, Madrid/Bridgeman Art Library; pages 62–63: Palacio del Senado, Madrid/Bridgeman Art Library; page 64: Victoria and Albert Museum/Bridgeman Art Library; page 65: Werner Forman/Art Resource NY; page 66: Index/Bridgeman Art Library

Contents

A Marriage Changes History

Spain in
Isabel ar

Together, modern Spain and Portugal form the
Iberian Peninsula. Today, the region is an easily
accessible haven for tourists seeking sunny beaches
and historic sites. But in the Middle Ages, travel
into and out of the Peninsula was difficult. The
soaring, snow-covered peaks of the Pyrenees
Mountains that separate Spain from France were a
formidable barrier to anyone trying to enter or
leave the country. To the south, the Sierra Nevada
Mountains blocked access to the Mediterranean
Sea, and the west faced the unknown waters of the
Atlantic Ocean. Fertile land was to be found
mainly along the coastline and in the south and
east. The central region of the Peninsula consisted
of a high, arid plateau, known as the Meseta—an
infertile, hostile environment, broken up by rough
mountain ranges.

This rugged geography naturally divided the

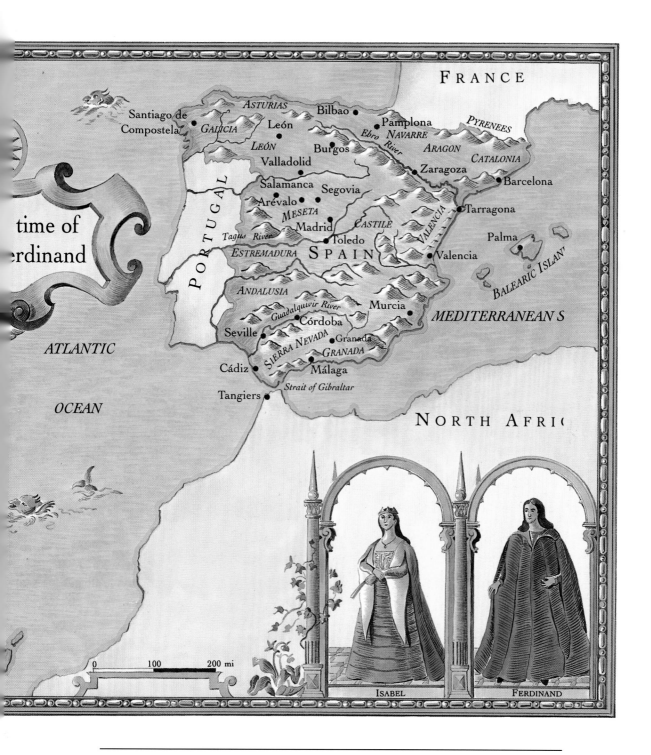

time of
rdinand

FRANCE

PYRENEES

Santiago de
Compostela

GALICIA

ASTURIAS

Bilbao

León

Pamplona
NAVARRE

Ebro
River

ARAGON

CATALONIA

P O R T U G A L

Burgos

Valladolid

Salamanca

Segovia

Zaragoza

Barcelona

Arévalo

MESETA

Madrid

CASTILE

Tarragona

VALENCIA

Tagus River

Toledo

ESTREMADURA

S P A I N

Palma

BALEARIC ISLAN

ANDALUSIA

Valencia

ATLANTIC

Guadalquivir River

Murcia

MEDITERRANEAN S

Córdoba

Seville

SIERRA NEVADA

Granada

OCEAN

GRANADA

Cádiz

Málaga

Tangiers

Strait of Gibraltar

N O R T H   A F R I (

0   100   200 mi

ISABEL   FERDINAND

Peninsula into several distinct regions, each with its own dialect and customs, and its own strong sense of independence. Throughout history, the boundaries of these territories were constantly changing. Periodically they expanded into provinces and kingdoms, formed alliances with neighbors, or broke down into smaller "counties." By the eleventh century, the kingdom of Castile, which occupied most of the Meseta, had absorbed the kingdom of León in the northwest. Aragon, in the northeast, had allied itself with Catalonia to become the dominant realm of the Peninsula. In a small territory between Castile and Aragon, bordering on France, lay the mountainous kingdom of Navarre. Spanning most of the western coast was the kingdom of Portugal. To the south lay the kingdom of Granada, which stood in lush and fertile contrast to the rest of Iberia.

Despite its difficult terrain, Spain's strategic location between Europe and Africa had attracted many conquerors over the centuries. Each new wave left its mark. The original Iberians had to fight hard to reclaim their lands from invading Celts, Greeks, and Carthaginians. In the third century B.C.E.*, the Romans invaded Iberia. They remained in power in their new province, which they called Hispania, for some six hundred years, eventually introducing Christianity to the area. Some of their many great works of engineering, such as the aqueducts and amphitheater of Mérida and the bridge of Córdoba, still stand today. The Latin language, which the Romans introduced, eventually became the basis for modern Spanish. But in the fifth century C.E., the

---

*Many systems of dating have been used by different cultures throughout history. This series of books uses B.C.E. (Before Common Era) and C.E. (Common Era) instead of B.C. (Before Christ) and A.D. (Anno Domini) out of respect for the diversity of the world's peoples.

Romans were in their turn conquered—this time by the Visigoths from Germany.

Meanwhile, events in far distant Arabia were creating a whirlwind that would affect the Iberian Peninsula forever. For centuries, the nomadic Bedouin tribes there had been pagans. Competition for survival in their harsh desert environment had involved them in endless blood feuds. In 610 C.E., however, in the Arabian city of Mecca, the prophet Muhammad founded the new religion of Islam, whose followers were known as Muslims. He preached that instead of worshipping many gods, Muslims had to submit to just one God, Allah. This new idea took fierce hold among the Bedouins, and helped to unite them in the achievement of one goal: the spread of Islam over the known world. Muslim armies ranged in all directions. Within one hundred years, the Muslim empire stretched from the western regions of India across Persia, Arabia, and Egypt and along the North African coast to include the modern nations of Tunisia, Algeria, and Morocco—just eight miles away from the Iberian shore.

During this period, the Visigoths' rule of the Iberian Peninsula had broken down into chaos, with individual families fighting for power. In 711 C.E., a claimant to the throne asked the Moroccan Muslims, whom the Christians called Moors, to help him overthrow the Visigothic king. Led by the governor of Tangiers, who saw an excellent opportunity to further the cause of Islam, the Moors eagerly crossed the narrow Strait of Gibraltar to reach al-Andalus—their name for the Peninsula. But they did not stop there. Iberia fell easy prey to their onrushing armies, which took a mere seven years to subjugate the Peninsula as far north as the Ebro River. The Moors were to remain for nearly eight hundred

Along with their religion, the Moors brought many advancements in learning to the Iberian Peninsula.

years. Their influence, more than that of any other invaders, would indelibly mark Spanish culture for centuries to come.

In stark contrast to the Moors' desert homelands, southern Spain—or Andalusia, as it came to be known—offered them a green and fertile paradise. In a short time, the city of Córdoba was established as the Moorish capital. Along with Islam, the Muslims brought a highly advanced civilization to their new home. Arab scholars had preserved learned writings from ancient Greece, Rome, and the Middle East, and Muslims were making great strides in architecture, mathematics, medicine, and science. They were also excellent farmers, artisans, and traders. Moorish goods such as glass, paper, leather, metalwork, and silk were renowned as far away as India. By the ninth century, the city of Córdoba had exploded into a metropolis of half a million citizens and boasted some eight hundred mosques; a university where science, medicine, and philosophy flourished, and a library that held four thousand volumes. In the thirteenth century, the province of Granada became the main Muslim kingdom, dominated by the magnificent Alhambra palace in the capital city, also called Granada.

The Alhambra palace in Granada was a combination palace and fortress, and the seat of Muslim royalty in Spain for several centuries. Its great courtyards, pools, and arched walkways made it a monument to Muslim architecture. Each lion around this famous fountain spouted water at a different hour of the day.

The Moorish influence in Spain was so strong that many Christians became Muslims and even made the traditional pilgrimage to Mecca, the holiest city of Islam. Muslim architecture dominated many cities. There were even brief periods of peaceful interaction between Christians and Muslims. But the majority of Christians saw Islam as the dark enemy of their faith. They also feared new invasions of Moors from North Africa, and never lost their determination to recapture southern Spain from the Muslims. From the start, the more powerful northern provinces that had escaped Moorish domination led successful raids against the Muslims. Little by little, they pushed southward. From other European countries, crusaders were attracted to the cause. With their help, it was the Castilians—perched on the Muslim front— who led the slow but relentless conquest of Muslim strongholds that became known as the *reconquista*. By 1248, after five hundred years of intermittent warfare, only the tiny kingdom of Granada remained in Muslim hands.

An added element to this boiling cauldron was the many Jews who had lived side by side with Christians on the Iberian Peninsula since the first century C.E. Throughout Europe, Christians had always subjected Jews to many laws regulating what they could or could not do, and Spain was no exception. When the Moors arrived, the Jews hoped for better times, for Jews and Muslims shared a long history. They had inhabited the same territories in the Middle East and North Africa for centuries and had much in common. Despite periods of anti-Semitism in Muslim regions, the Jews had long engaged in an exchange of learning with the Muslims. They even wrote Arabic using Hebrew characters. Under the Moors in Spain, their culture entered a

A Hebrew manuscript illustration shows Spanish Jews at worship, around 1350.

golden age of literature and philosophy, and they enjoyed a brief freedom from the persecution that had hounded them for centuries. They remained, however, a separate and mysterious culture to the Christians.

Embroiled in its own problems, Christian Iberia had long been poor. Then quite suddenly—as though a magic spell had been cast—Spain emerged in the late fifteenth century as the most powerful nation in the world! By this time, Castile had become the dominant kingdom. It was now identified by the rest of Europe as Spain, and its language as Spanish. By the mid-1500s, it would rule an empire that extended from Italy, Germany, and the Netherlands to the Caribbean, Florida, Mexico, Central America, and parts of South America. Untold wealth in silver and gold would flow into Spanish coffers while Spanish arts and letters would flourish as never before.

The catalyst that catapulted Spain into this sudden prominence was the marriage of Princess Isabel of Castile and Prince Ferdinand of Aragon in 1469. They were a supremely gifted couple with extraordinary political skills. Together, they forged the unification of Castile and Aragon, setting the stage for a great empire and paving the way for the modern nation of Spain. They are especially noted for the events of 1492. In this year, the monarchs finally drove out the Moors from Granada and sent Christopher Columbus on his monumental journey into the unknown. They were also responsible for the horrors of the Spanish Inquisition, in which thousands of people who did not follow the sovereigns' rigid Catholicism were tortured or killed. In 1492, they ordered the expulsion of all Jews from Spain.

In this book, you will learn about Isabel and Ferdinand's

Isabel and Ferdinand were so devout, they became known as the Catholic Monarchs.

extraordinary reign. You will discover how the Spanish people lived and thought during that time. And, through their letters, edicts, chronicles, ballads, and poems, you will experience first-hand the words of these powerful rulers and their subjects.

PART ONE

Isabel and Ferdinand loved pomp and ceremony. The public looked forward to their frequent processions, or parades, which served as religious and political spectacles.

Much as the Other"

Isabel of Castile: The Princess

Isabel came from a long line of Catholic kings and queens who firmly believed that royalty was a God-given gift. The position of queen came with unrestricted privilege as well as a strong sense of duty. Born in 1451, Isabel spent her early years at Arévalo, a market town in the heart of the Castilian Meseta. Her mother became depressed or, some say, mad, soon after Isabel's birth, and locked herself away in a dark room of their castle. When Isabel was three, her father, King Juan II, died and her half brother Enrique IV became king. He visited Arévalo frequently and kept a close eye on Isabel and her younger brother, Alfonso. But it was mainly Isabel's grandmother, Isabel de Barcelos, who ran the household. This formidable woman was of royal Portuguese stock and certainly impressed the young Isabel with her quality of no-nonsense regal authority.

While growing up, Isabel had also been exposed to various heroes and heroines of history. Castilians were a hardy breed of people who had to be tough to weather the blistering summers and icy winters of their Meseta. So it is not surprising that they revered the great Roman emperors Hadrian and Trajan, who were born in Spain. Isabel's father had also greatly admired Joan of Arc. This famous fifteenth-century heroine was only seventeen

A friend of Isabel's described her as "the handsomest lady whom I ever beheld." She was of middle height and had a fair complexion, chestnut hair, and blue eyes. Her soft voice and modest manner hid a will of steel.

when she led French troops to victory against the English; she was later burned at the stake as a heretic. The Castilian warrior Rodrigo Díaz de Vivar, known as El Cid, had led the struggle against the Moors in the eleventh century, and was often held up as a role model for the Castilian character.

Isabel would also have heard tales of glory from the many retired soldiers, or conquistadores, who guarded the castle. Their ballads and legends told of brave deeds in the Spanish civil wars, in northern Africa, the Canary Islands, and Portugal. It was from them, perhaps, that Isabel heard tales of fabulous African kingdoms rich in gold, of slaves, of strange new lands with exotic names. It was a time of new frontiers as the adventurous Castilians looked to expand their territories to the south, in Africa, and to the north, in Europe. Many of these soldiers had spent their lives fighting in the *reconquista*, which had gone on for so long that fighting had become a Castilian way of life. So, like all other Castilians of the time, Isabel naturally accepted war and glorified warriors.

Thus, although Isabel was taught "womanly" skills such as sewing and singing, she also absorbed the values of the strong men and women who played leading roles in her life. She later became known for her strength of will and extraordinary self-control. Hernando del Pulgar, Isabel's secretary when she was queen, recorded that even in childbirth, "she was able to mask her feelings and betray not a sign or expression of the pain which all women suffer." It is also recorded that she enjoyed hunting and once killed a savage bear with her own javelin.

Europe at the time was steeped in the religious fervor of Christianity. Isabel's grandmother, Isabel de Barcelos, was a devout Catholic who often made pilgrimages in her bare feet to certain shrines. Her young ward was an intelligent, well-read woman whose life revolved entirely around her faith. Princess Isabel's days were marked by the chiming of church bells, the strictly held periods of prayer, and the annual cycle of holy days and feasts. As an adult, she would outdo her grandmother in religious matters and would, in fact, become known in history as the Catholic Queen—the most devout of all.

Ferdinand of Aragon: The Prince

Ferdinand was born in 1452, in the town of Sos in Aragon. From the first, his mother raised him to be a king and an exemplary Catholic. She even postponed his baptism for nearly a year, waiting until the infant's succession to the throne could not be questioned. Then the baptismal ceremony was held in the great cathedral at Zaragoza, with all the pomp and ceremony the kingdom could muster.

While Castile was landlocked and rather isolated, Aragon was directly in touch with the Mediterranean world. Along its coastline, ports such as Barcelona and Valencia thrived. From them, an extensive network of overseas trading connections linked Aragon with France, Italy, Greece, and North Africa. As a child, Ferdinand would have been exposed to the many different peoples and wares coming and going from these ports. Perhaps these early influences helped to develop his later flair for international politics.

Twice, Ferdinand had been very ill as a child. But as a youth, he was immensely strong and healthy. Unlike most children of the time, he was taught to read and write and from the age of ten had commanded his own staff of retainers and soldiers. Like all young knights, he had been rigorously trained in horsemanship and weaponry. He loved to joust—and also to gamble. While he was

From the time he was a boy, Ferdinand held positions of power. As he grew older, he was considered brave, energetic, and adventurous.

A ducat, or gold coin, minted during the time of Ferdinand I, who was king of Aragon from 1412 to 1416.

not an intellectual, he was curious about everything and always eager to learn. Poetry, lectures, and stories served to instruct Ferdinand in the morals and religious principles of the time.

Prince Ferdinand was a good-looking young man. It is said that "he had so singular a grace that everyone who talked to him wanted to serve him." As he grew older, he proved extremely attractive to the ladies, and fathered four illegitimate children. At the same time, Ferdinand was a devout Catholic. Every morning before breakfast, he attended mass. On Maundy Thursday, his servants would find twelve of the poorest of his subjects so that Ferdinand could serve them supper and wash their feet—just as Jesus had done with his disciples.

When Ferdinand was five, his father, Juan II, had become king. At a very early age, Ferdinand had already shown remarkable skills in leadership and politics. By the age of nine, he had been named governor of one of his father's kingdoms. Ferdinand acted as his father's right hand in matters at home while the king waged war against France. In 1462, civil war broke out in Aragon. Businessmen and merchants, who disagreed with the king's policies on trade, raised armies to overthrow King Juan. At the age of twelve, Prince Ferdinand led royal forces in battle against these enemies of his father, and won. From then on, he was the darling of Aragon, a hero who had the full support of his people.

Although Aragon participated in the fight to drive out the Moors, the kingdom was not quite so determined in this goal as Castile was. The Aragonese were a seafaring people. By the time Ferdinand became king in 1479, Aragon already possessed a Mediterranean empire that included the Balearic Islands just off the Spanish coast, as well as Sardinia and Sicily, islands off the coast of Italy. As king, Ferdinand had to not only maintain control over his territories but also expand them.

One of Ferdinand's most important advisers was Joan Margarit, the bishop of Gerona. Margarit counseled that before Aragon could be strong abroad, the kingdom had to be secure at home. The nobility in Aragon had far greater power than the Crown, and as a result there was frequent warfare. In order to bring peace to the land, the bishop believed, Aragon would need a strong king, one who could navigate the complex web of intrigues and power moves that riddled the nobility. It would take cunning, said the bishop. A king needed to rule with wisdom, rather than with a strict moral code. A king might make promises that he need not keep.

It seems that Ferdinand listened well to his teacher. In later years, he gained a reputation for cunning; some chroniclers even called him devious. The Spanish monarch became universally recognized as a shrewd and brilliant manipulator of people and politics.

The Royal Family

Isabel did not come easily to the throne of Castile. King Enrique was determined that his "daughter" Juana (it was suspected that he was not really her father) should inherit the throne. He did everything possible to prevent first his half brother Alfonso and then Isabel from becoming successors. The kingdom, viciously divided over the issue, erupted into civil war. After Alfonso's sudden death in 1468—he may have been murdered by one of Enrique's allies—Isabel felt that she was the natural successor to her father's throne, and she found many supporters to her claim.

Isabel knew she had a better chance of becoming queen if she were married, but not to any of the suitors whom Enrique had in mind. She had secretly sent her own chaplain to look over potential husbands—always with the political future of Castile in mind. He had returned with a glowing description of Ferdinand, saying that the prince was "very gallant, handsome in countenance, body and person, and of noble air." Isabel's choice was clear: she would marry the prince of Aragon who was, in fact, a cousin. She had support from several Spanish leaders, who had long hoped for an alliance between the two kingdoms.

Things moved fast. Ferdinand's father, King Juan, was delighted at the match because it would greatly increase the power and wealth of Aragon. Meanwhile, Enrique forbade Prince Ferdinand—on pain of death—to set foot on Castilian soil. But nothing could stop the turn of events now. In the fall of 1469, Ferdinand left Aragon disguised as a servant and rode through the hostile countryside with a few retainers. On the night of October 14, pro-Isabel nobles led Ferdinand to the room where she waited. She was eighteen, auburn haired, with steady eyes and a regal bearing. He was seventeen, flaxen haired, with sparkling eyes and a muscular body. Within two hours, they had agreed to marry and four days later, the wedding took place—without King Enrique. It was to prove an excellent marriage and political partnership. As Isabel developed her considerable skills in internal politics, Ferdinand was to prove a master at foreign affairs.

The terms of the union were carefully worked out by politicians on both sides. Ferdinand would inherit the throne of Aragon when his father died. In Castile, although he was Isabel's husband, or consort, he would not become king as long as Isabel or any of their children lived. If the throne fell to a son or daughter who was too young or otherwise incapable of ruling, Ferdinand would become the regent, or effective ruler. Aragon was much smaller than Castile*, and in effect, Ferdinand's position would be far weaker than his wife's. He had to promise to obey King Enrique, to appoint only Castilians to office, to observe Castile's laws and customs, and not to remove Isabel or any of their children from Castile. However, he and Isabel would make all decisions together. Initially, Ferdinand was upset at his lesser role, but Isabel was extremely diplomatic. She assured him that, privately, they would share equal power. What was not written in law they would make

*Historians estimate that Castile had a population of around seven million, and Aragon about three million.

up for through love and trust. Together, they developed a motto: *tanto monta, monta tanto*—"the one as much as the other."

King Enrique died and Isabel became queen of Castile in 1474. When Ferdinand became king of Aragon five years later, it was fully expected that, despite his marriage agreement, he would become the true ruler of Castile. But everyone had underestimated Isabel, for it was she who took the reins and proved herself by far the more powerful authority.

Children, Marriage, and Power

One of the royal couple's main goals was to create and cement strong political ties to the most powerful European nations. In the tradition of European royalty, this was achieved through their children's marriages.

Their first child, Isabel, was born in 1470. Ferdinand was disappointed, for he longed for a son to inherit the throne. His dream came true in 1478, when Isabel gave birth to a boy whom they named Juan. To build long-lasting ties with Austria's powerful Habsburg family, it was arranged that Juan would marry Margaret, daughter of Austria's Emperor Maximilian. One year later, another daughter, Juana, was born. Like Isabel's mother, this child was depressed or insane, and went down in history as Juana the Mad. Nevertheless, she married Maximilian's son Philip I, and their son, Charles V, became ruler of the vast territories of the Holy Roman Empire. Two more girls followed: Maria, who later became queen of Portugal, and Catalina, who married England's King Henry VIII.

In 1490, Princess Isabel married Portugal's Prince Afonso, heir

Juana the Mad. Like her maternal grandmother, she was given to bouts of severe depression.

to that throne. Sadly, only six months later, Afonso was killed in a riding accident and young Isabel—half dead with sorrow—returned to Castile. Greater tragedies were to follow. In 1497, Prince Juan—much beloved by the Castilians and well trained to become king—died suddenly of a fever. Only a year later, the widowed Isabel, who had married again, died in childbirth. Her parents' only consolation was the fact that her son, Miguel, could inherit the throne. They invested all their hopes in him, but he was sickly and died at the age of two. After all their efforts, this left Juana the Mad next in line to the throne of Spain.

The Spanish Inquisition

During the Middle Ages (from about 500 to 1500 C.E.), the Catholic Church, under the rule of the pope in Rome, was a powerful force in Europe. The teachings of the church were regarded as the foundation of law and order. Christians who did not agree with Catholic doctrine were considered heretics, and heresy was regarded as an offense against the state as well as the church. Over the years there were numerous occasions when the church sought out, questioned, and punished heretics. These "inquiries" into a person's faith became known as the Inquisition. The goal was to educate the individual and bring him or her "back into the fold." Usually, the inquisitors were priests or bishops who subjected a suspect to long interrogations followed by terrible tortures. Death by fire was often the punishment for those who did not repent. The heretic's property was then claimed by the church.

By the time Isabel and Ferdinand came to power, the Inquisition had long been active elsewhere on the Continent. The sovereigns were devout—some say fanatical—Catholics. Like other European leaders at the time, they believed that religious unity would foster political unity. In other words, there was no distinction between "church" and "state." Thus Isabel dreamed of achieving "spiritual purity" among her people, and in this, she was heavily influenced by her religious adviser, Tomás de Torquemada. He warned her that "in these kingdoms are many blasphemers, renegades from God and the Saints." Torquemada was referring to the Jews, whom he loathed. Many Jews were merchants who traveled all the known trade routes of the world. Through international trade, a class of wealthy Jewish bankers had emerged who came to play a vital role in the Spanish economy. But the Jews were not only merchants and financiers; they were also physicians, educators, and counselors to the royal courts.

Torquemada especially hated those Jews who had converted to Catholicism and were known as *conversos*, or "new Christians." Many of these *conversos* were wealthy and held powerful positions at court. It was said that they only pretended to be Catholics while secretly practicing Judaism, and this raised the level of mistrust against them. Anti-Semitism had flared up frequently in Spain over the centuries, and Torquemada now fanned the flames again. To achieve religious purity, Spain had to be rid of *conversos*! With this goal, he persuaded the sovereigns to request that Pope Sixtus IV in Rome bring the Inquisition to Spain. Initially, Isabel was reluctant. But Ferdinand saw an opportunity to swell the royal treasury with property and money confiscated from these wealthy people. And thus the wheels of the Inquisition began to turn.

Isabel appointed Torquemada as the Grand Inquisitor, and he selected five men to sit in judgment with him on the High Council. The High Council made all decisions concerning the Inquisition and set up several lower courts around the country. The members of the High Council developed rules to ensure that the accused received a "fair" trial. The accused, for example, were

The accused, marked by their conical hats, stand out as figures of shame in this scene of the Inquisition, re-created by the famous Spanish artist Goya, around 1794.

given the services of a lawyer, and two impartial priests had to be present at the trials.

Wearing white robes with black hoods, the inquisitors first arrived in Seville in October 1480. Their method was to announce a "pardon" of thirty to forty days, during which "heretics," who had usually been denounced by other citizens, were supposed to come forward and "confess." If they did, these penitents had to wear a coarse woolen robe, called a *sanbenito*, and a foolish conical hat, marking them as objects of disgust. Those who did not repent went to trial. All were assumed guilty until proved innocent. No one—rich or poor, male or female, adult or child—was spared.

Immediately, there were riots and thousands of *conversos* and others who believed themselves in danger fled to other parts of Europe. They abandoned their properties and businesses. Soon after they left, the economy of the region began to decline. Then, in January 1481, an edict was issued in Seville requiring everyone's help in the accusation and arrest of suspected heretics. To save their own lives, people accused others until there were soon thousands of victims held for trial. On January 6, six men and women were burned at the stake in the first public auto-da-fé, or "act of faith," intended to show the power of church and state and to intimidate further "offenders."

Over the course of eight years in Seville alone, seven hundred people—mostly *conversos*—were burned alive and five thousand more were imprisoned for life. Even the bones of those long dead but suspected of heresy were dug up and publicly burned. Their children were forbidden to hold any important office and their property was confiscated and added to the royal inventory. The pattern was repeated throughout Spain. As the Inquisition gathered momentum, it began to interfere in every aspect of daily life. People could be arrested and "tried" for subversive words, thoughts, and writings; for sexual misbehavior; for anything, in short, that seemed suspicious. Books that were considered heretical were banned and burned. Laws were passed, called the *limpieza de sangre*, or "purity of blood" laws, which forbade anyone with the slightest hint of Moorish or Jewish blood from seeking office or marrying a Christian.

There were small pockets of Jewish resistance. In Aragon, an inquisitor was murdered. But the accomplices suffered such savage deaths that no one else dared to act. Soon spies were turning in "evildoers" to save their own lives, and fear and terror ruled the land. Worse was to come. On March 31, 1492, the sovereigns signed an edict giving all Jews in Spain four months to accept baptism or be expelled from the country. The Jews' attempts to buy or persuade their way out of this nightmare failed. Many—in absolute despair—accepted baptism. By August, the rest—perhaps 100,000 Jews*—had fled.

The Inquisition did not end there. Isabel and Ferdinand had never forgotten their pledge to rid Spain of the Muslims remaining in Granada. The Inquisition made their dream of achieving "spiritual purity" in Spain all the more justifiable. Thus, with doubled purpose, Ferdinand had waged war against the kingdom of Granada for eleven years. For a full year, he besieged the city of Granada. Finally, on January 2, 1492, with his people dying of starvation, the Muslim ruler Muhammad XI, known to the Spanish as Boabdil, had to surrender. The *reconquista* was over.

Captured Muslims had always been kept as slaves. Now Spain's landed noblemen appealed to Isabel. They feared that, if Muslims were forced to leave the country, they might lose their slave labor and hence their profits. Instead of expelling the Muslims, therefore, the Christians began to force Muslims to convert. Children were separated from their families and given to the church to be

---

*Some historians give numbers as high as 800,000, others as low as 50,000.

Boabdil secretly negotiated the surrender of Granada with the monarchs' envoys. He handed over the keys to the palace and sighed in grief as he left his kingdom. A hill near Granada is called The Last Sigh of the Moor.

Isabel and Ferdinand entered Granada in royal splendor. Among their soldiers were many Christian volunteers from other countries, who wished to help conquer the Muslims. In Rome, the pope held a high mass in celebration.

raised as Christians. Muslims were forbidden to speak Arabic—often the only language they knew. Converted Muslims, who were known as Moriscos, were carefully watched to ensure that no vestige of Muslim practices remained. In 1502, Isabel did issue a decree offering the few remaining Muslims the "choice" between baptism or expulsion. In reality, however, Spain could not afford to lose its workforce and few were allowed to leave. Those who could, including Boabdil, went to North Africa. In Spain, Islam was virtually stamped out. To add to the mayhem, there was an outbreak of disease on the Peninsula and many people died. All these events left Spain's population decimated, its farms and cities virtually empty.

The Inquisition brought all kingdoms and peoples of Spain under one yoke, but at a tremendous price. At one blow, Spain lost both Muslim and Jewish culture, talent, taxes, and business, leaving the region devastated and impoverished right into modern times. The Inquisition was to continue into the nineteenth century, leaving a permanent mark on Spain and its people.

The New World

In the midst of these momentous events, Christopher Columbus had settled in Seville, hoping to persuade the Spanish sovereigns to finance his journey across the Atlantic. Ferdinand's attention was directed toward expanding his territories in Europe, so it was mainly Isabel who showed an interest in Columbus's ideas.

Isabel, who was considered one of the most important personages in Europe, was ambitious to extend Castilian authority—and Christianity—farther abroad. She also recognized the need for an alternative trade route to the East, since the traditional overland routes passed through Muslim lands. Portugal had begun its rapid expansion in Africa, where it laid claim to gold, slaves, and other riches. Spain was anxious not to be left behind in the race to exploit these new worlds. Most of all, Isabel hoped that Columbus would find Prester John, the fabled Christian king who was supposed to live somewhere in the East and who would help Christians reclaim the holy city of Jerusalem from the Muslims.

Columbus's daring leap across the Atlantic Ocean in 1492 was the culmination of everything Spain had known up to that point. The Spanish loved to travel and had been expanding their territories and resettling new areas for centuries. Technology and ship design were ready for the future and this was just one more great adventure. In Columbus's wake came thousands of colonists*, most of whom were Castilians, who brought their language to the Americas. The form of government, church practices, the Inquisition, slavery, even the building of cities—which most Spaniards preferred over the countryside—and the idea of the supreme power of the monarchy were also exported to the New World. During the *reconquista*, the Castilians had practiced a policy of military conquest followed by the immediate occupancy of the conquered land by settlers. This pattern later became standard in the New World, where settlers were given land grants and native or African slaves, whom they promised to Christianize.

People in Spain were fascinated by the new foods coming from the Americas, such as corn and potatoes, and by the Indians Columbus brought back with him. Yet, mainly because the Spanish monarchs were in debt to European financiers, who were anxious to get back their initial investments, Spain's focus in the New World very soon became the search for precious metals. Native Americans and, later, Africans were ruthlessly exploited as slaves in the mines and before long, Spain was enjoying a steady flow of silver and gold

*Until Isabel's death, only Castilians could travel freely to America. All other Spaniards had to gain special permission.

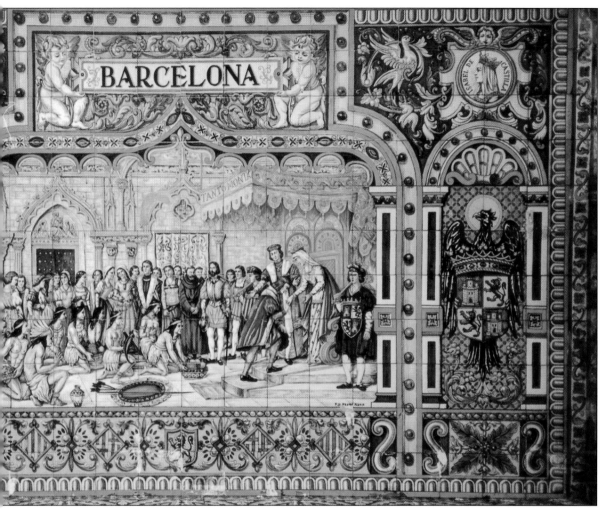

Columbus shows products from the New World to the Spanish monarchs.
Several Native Americans were also presented to the court.

into the coffers at Seville. When gold and silver deposits in one area of the Americas were exhausted, the Spanish simply conquered another. Ferdinand set up an extremely complex bureaucracy to create and maintain a monopoly over imports and exports to the Americas. Every shipload was jealously guarded and no other

Native Americans died quickly from European diseases brought by the Spanish to the Americas. African slaves were hardier and lived longer.

nations were permitted to trade with the colonies. Ferdinand was not interested in encouraging trade and industry; his goal was solely to increase revenues to the Crown.

The web of family connections with the Habsburgs and other powerful royal families of Europe reduced the possibility of threats to Spanish territories. This freed up vast resources that could be directed toward the creation of a huge empire. Before Columbus's voyage to the Americas, Spain's only important possession outside Europe was the Canary Islands. By the mid–sixteenth century, however, Spain would control most of the Caribbean, including Puerto Rico, Jamaica, and Cuba. Spanish conquistadores would defeat the Aztec and Inca empires, extending Spanish holdings from Florida and Mexico down through Venezuela, Peru, and Chile. Spain would become prosperous as never before. For almost a century, its military power and tremendous wealth would give the nation a position of absolute supremacy in Europe and the territories it governed. This new wealth would trigger an explosion of learning in the arts and sciences, architecture, law, and other fields. In short, Spain would enter an era that has gone down in its history as its Golden Age.

Despite the extraordinary wealth that poured into Spain, the Catholic Monarchs' shortsighted economic planning eventually paved the way to ruin. Ferdinand and Isabel relied entirely on imports of gold and silver, rather than on trade and industry, to finance their policies. After one hundred years, the mines in the Americas would run dry and financial disaster would hit. By the end of the sixteenth century, Spain would begin its long decline.

The End of an Era

When Isabel's grandson Miguel died, Marineo Sículo, a court chronicler, wrote, "Such great grief has swept over . . . the whole court that no one has been able to approach the Queen, for the King and the Queen are bowed down in deep distress." What they suffered privately, Isabel and Ferdinand hid from the public. Wars were waged, ships were sent across the far seas, and matters at home and abroad were dealt with. Yet their suffering took its toll. Isabel became ill and ruled from her bed for a few months. In 1504, she wrote her last will. She was sure of life eternal in heaven and wanted to absolve herself of all sin or blame before she got there. Among other things, money was to be given to the poor. Her debts were to be paid, and twenty thousand masses were to be said. On November 26, at the age of fifty-three, Isabel received the last sacraments, sighed, and died peacefully. Ferdinand was distraught and wrote that "she was the best and most excellent wife that ever a king had, the sorrow of the absence of her is ripping my entrails."

Despite his grief, Ferdinand married again two years later. He was still only the regent in Castile, but his daughter Juana was mentally ill and deemed unfit to rule. Her husband, Philip I, died in 1506. Thus Ferdinand became king of Castile, adding this to all his other titles.

In the winter of 1515, Ferdinand was stricken with fever. He lost interest in politics and became severely depressed. In his last will, he requested that he lie next to Isabel in the cathedral at Granada, as they had both desired. Ferdinand died on January 23, 1516, aged sixty-four, leaving behind a vast empire to his grandson, Holy Roman Emperor Charles V.

The monarchs' grandchildren: Charles I of Spain (Holy Roman Emperor Charles V) with his brother (*on the left*) and sisters.

Evaluating Isabel and Ferdinand

In order to understand Isabel and Ferdinand, a modern reader must try to place them firmly in their times. Today, we value tolerance of other people's viewpoints and religious beliefs. We do not try to make everyone conform to a single standard of beliefs and behavior. In Isabel and Ferdinand's times, religion was a powerful unifying force. For hundreds of years, the Catholic Church in Rome had ruled Europe, bringing order to the continent after the chaos that followed the fall of the Roman Empire in the fifth century.

Both monarchs believed in John the Evangelist's New Testament prophecy that God planned to bring the world to an end. It would be renewed, he said, by a warrior-king, or Messiah, who would usher in a golden age of peace. Isabel and Ferdinand believed that this king would be chosen by God from their own royal family and that, in order to fulfill the prophecy, the Spanish race had to be pure. Thus, in their eyes, God would favor the expulsion of such "unclean" elements as Jews and Muslims. God would also support Christian efforts to conquer and convert non-Christians, no matter how brutally these victories were won.

Although Isabel and Ferdinand often caused great suffering, they almost always had good intentions and firmly believed that they were acting in the best interests of their subjects and their realm. Their actions were not only accepted but lauded by other European rulers. In fact, some historians now maintain that our information on the Inquisition is exaggerated based on propaganda written around 1567 by anti-Catholic Protestants. Today, some of the Catholic Sovereigns' deeds are viewed as barbaric; others as heroic. Yet their work sowed the seeds from which Spain's Golden Age was able to flower.

Everyday Life

In this idealized scene of peasant life, workers take a break from the heavy labor of harvesting wheat.

Fifteenth-Century Spain

Government

Castilian kings through the ages had traditionally gathered with the clergy and the nobility for advice on important matters. These meetings were known as the Cortes. Abbots, bishops, and archbishops, called the "first estate," automatically held positions in the Cortes. The "second estate" was made up of the most influential dukes and nobles, the officers of the Crown, and wealthy landowners. By the twelfth century, a "third estate" consisting of deputies from important towns, who represented the citizens, had been added to the Cortes. Originally, the Cortes had tremendous power. It met at least once a year and was consulted on matters such as foreign policy and royal marriages, the import and export of goods, the protection of agriculture, and many other concerns. But Isabel and Ferdinand's main goal was to increase the power of the Crown, which could only be achieved by reducing the power of the Cortes.

At the top of the Castilian social hierarchy were the few great families that comprised the "second estate" of the Cortes. They had been given most of the land taken from the Moors and, with their great wealth, exercised enormous political power. The Castilian monarchy had, in fact, become pawns in their hands. This caused such turmoil over the succession to the throne that civil war raged from 1474 to 1479. It was only after Isabel's victory in this war that she and Ferdinand were able to curb the power of the aristocracy and thus of the Cortes.

Isabel and Ferdinand administer justice in one of the many courts they held around the country.

Funds allocated by the Cortes were raised from taxes. Since the nobility and the clergy did not have to pay taxes, they often had little interest in attending the meetings. The sovereigns cleverly used the absence of these officials to undermine their authority. Another strategy was to convene sessions at the monarchs' own whim, usually when they desperately needed money for war or other expensive projects. The rest of the time, they tended to ignore this great institution, once even allowing a gap of sixteen years without a meeting.

To further cement the Crown's power, the monarchs entirely reorganized the government so that it worked more closely through their royal authority. Their main tools were royal councils, which were in attendance at court throughout the year. These were the Councils of State, Justice, Finances, the Inquisition, the Military, the Indies, and the Hermandad.* This last council gave the monarchs control over the towns. They also won control over the church by winning from the pope the right to select church authorities.

In Aragon, each of the kingdom's highly independent provinces was administered by its own Cortes, since it was considered impossible for the king to rule such a diverse empire. While the landowners in Aragon were wealthy and powerful, the real masters of the kingdom were the merchants and businessmen who dominated economic life. They arranged a contract between the king and his subjects, and added a "fourth estate" to their Cortes—that of ordinary gentlemen—which gave the people greater representation. They won legislation requiring that laws could only be made or repealed by mutual consent of the king and the Cortes. For this reason, Ferdinand avoided the Cortes as often as possible. He knew, for example, that the members of the institution might not award him funds for his various wars. So he would raise soldiers through his own means and then saddle the kingdom with the cost of their support. Eventually, however,

---

*Prior to the monarchs' rule, Castile had been overrun with criminals and life everywhere was extremely dangerous. To combat this problem, each town formed a *hermandad*, or "brotherhood," that united the citizens of the town and created alliances with other towns. Its purpose was to guard the roads and mete out justice to thieves, rapists, murderers, and other criminals, especially in rural areas and distant hamlets.

despite its strong resistance, even the Aragonese Cortes buckled before royal power.

In the end, Isabel and Ferdinand united the various kingdoms of Spain by ruthlessly insisting on the supreme power of the Crown, which held authority above all other institutions. They created order where once chaos had existed, and unity where discord had been the rule. But the people of Spain lost much of their liberty and a potentially powerful democratic institution when the Cortes lost its authority.

Education

In the 1470s, the printing press with movable type, which had been invented in Germany, was introduced in Spain. Before, books and papers had been copied by hand—a very time-consuming and expensive process. While a scribe could perhaps complete one handwritten copy of a book in a year, a printer could turn out a thousand copies of the same book in the same amount of time. Excited about this breakthrough in technology, Isabel and Ferdinand passed a new law that allowed the tax-free importation of foreign books.

At the same time, Latin, the language of only the learned in society, was giving way to Castilian, the everyday language of the people. Isabel commissioned Antonio de Nebrija to compile the first Latin-Spanish dictionary, which was completed in 1492. The impact of these new developments was enormous. Now those who could read had access to the ideas of poets, philosophers, doctors, and scientists from other countries. The world was opening up, and Spain was an eager student.

Isabel and Ferdinand set the stage for a great flowering of culture and learning. With the monarchs' support, old universities like those in Salamanca and Valladolid gained new energy, while more than thirty new universities sprang up in other towns. Salamanca accepted both men and women, rich and poor, and there were even some female professors. It was here that

The University at Salamanca was progressive for its time and attracted students from all over the world.

Columbus revealed the secrets of the New World. Here, medical students were allowed to dissect the human body, which was forbidden almost everywhere else. Copernicus's discovery that the planets revolve around the sun was taught at Salamanca while it was still regarded as heresy elsewhere. In the city of Alcalá, the university boasted some three thousand students and became most famous for its Greek and Hebrew editions of the Old Testament.

Some chroniclers of the period complained that so many students were graduating from the universities that there were not enough jobs to keep them employed! Others noted that many "teachers" were ignorant. Nevertheless, Spain blossomed during the 1500s as never before or since. Advanced Spanish ship design and mapmaking took explorers to the far corners of the earth. Great thinkers produced major works on philosophy, religion, economics, and political theory; historians found more scientific ways of looking at the past; and Spanish authors were recognized as authorities on medicine, navigation, mining, metallurgy, and mineralogy. New forms of literature burst onto the market, paving the way for geniuses such as Cervantes, the author of the famous novel *Don Quixote*, and Lope de Vega, Spain's greatest dramatist. By the mid–sixteenth century, Spain was considered the center of learning in Europe.

The Moors designed this sophisticated, and beautiful, navigational tool—the astrolabe—around 1300.

The Spanish Conquistador

Spain could not have won its global territories without its soldiers, known as conquistadores, or "conquerors." The conquistadores were "men of iron"—it was said they could win any trial of endurance and were almost never defeated in battle.

There were many reasons for this reputation. First of all, Spain's rough terrain and uncomfortable climate—with freezing winters and blazing summers—bred hardy men who were not bothered by extremes of heat and cold. They rarely became sick. While French soldiers died by the thousands in America's malaria-ridden swamps, the Spaniards barely noticed. The Spanish soldier was not very interested in excesses of food and drink, and could easily survive on the bare minimum. He also reacted less emotionally than his French or Italian counterparts to victory or defeat. The conquistador was often a seafaring man and may have journeyed north to England and the Netherlands, or east across the Mediterranean, or with any of the great explorers to the Americas or the farther regions of Africa. So he was used to new sights and could quite easily adapt to new ways of life. Religious faith was his driving force, and the hopes of becoming wealthy from the spoils of war. In attaining these goals, he possessed an unparalleled discipline.

Francisco Pizarro
was one of Spain's
most famous
conquistadores,
best remembered
for his conquest of
the Inca Empire.

Because of the long struggle against the Moors, the Spanish
were raised from childhood to honor and admire the exploits of
their forefathers in battle. Fed a constant diet of stories about
chivalrous knights and brave warriors, they grew up already
ambitious to prove their strength, their loyalty, and their
manliness on the battlefield. To die defending Spain and its
sovereigns was considered a great honor.

Architecture and Design

The majority of people on the Iberian Peninsula lived in towns in simple houses built of packed mud, which were often washed away in heavy rains. The streets were rough paths with no paving. In the winter, they became muddy sewers; in the summer, people moved in a cloud of dust. Only the great castles and churches stood aloof in all their stony grandeur, built to last forever.

Before the reign of Isabel and Ferdinand, the Moors had had the greatest influence on Spanish architecture. They loved ornate carving and colorful tiles decorated with complex patterns. Their houses boasted intricate woodwork, balconies, and thick walls that kept rooms cool in the summer and warm in the winter. Ceilings were painted or carved, and magnificent archways led from one room to another. The Moors also created beautiful gardens, often irrigated with pools, fountains, and waterfalls, which were havens of peace in a rugged countryside. Where Christians surrounded themselves with religious images and statuary, Muslim law forbade any replication of Allah, the Arabic name for God. Thus Muslims became masters of purely decorative design, using flowers, animals, birds, and geometric patterns to enhance their surroundings.

Isabel and Ferdinand stamped their reign with a new kind of architecture. Before their time, churches and cathedrals had been

This room, with its fantastic designs in wood and tile, is a great example of Muslim decorative design. Built in the fourteenth century, it is part of the baths of the Alhambra.

rather severe in design, with little ornamentation. Isabel encouraged artisans to give free rein to their imagination, and a new style, called Isabelline, began to emerge. Flowers, fruit, foliage, animals, and imaginary creatures covered every available inch of stone on the facades of buildings. Carved like jewelry, fountains, pillars, arcades, and courtyards reflected the mix of Christian and Moorish tastes.

A flurry of building also reflected the new age of prosperity. More than seven hundred bridges were constructed in Castile and Aragon, making travel much easier. Architects started work on new cathedrals in Salamanca and Segovia. Other houses of worship, such as those in Burgos and Seville, which had been under construction for centuries, were pushed to completion. Many other projects celebrated military victories or simply the great power and self-confidence of the sovereigns.

During Enrique IV's reign, chaos had ruled the provinces of Spain and art was far from anyone's mind. But in the new era, it was as though the creative spirit of the Spaniards—especially the Castilians—had been repressed for centuries and suddenly came to life. Just as architecture now flourished, so did sculpture. Artists worked in marble, alabaster, and rare metals, taking sculpture to new heights. They knew how to make such hard materials resemble lace and velvet, and they duplicated every detail of clothing, jewelry, and hair with incredible skill. Isabel employed the sculptor Gil de Siloe to build the stone mausoleum, or tomb, of her father, mother, and younger brother. Other artists, such as Felipe de Borgona and Alonso Berruguete, were equally skilled with wood and carved church pews and choir stalls. Some of these works are considered among the finest of their kind in the world.

Food and Lodging

Many accounts report on the dismal conditions facing the traveler through fifteenth-century Spain. Robert Gauguin was a French priest employed on diplomatic missions between France and Spain. He wrote that most "rooms" were of mud, often infested with lice and other vermin. A traveler was provided with a clay dish, but had to find his own food and serve it up himself. Gauguin had to gather his own firewood and clean out the cooking pots he used. He also had to purchase hay and oats for his mule and tend to the animal himself. On top of all this, an innkeeper could charge whatever he wanted and prices were often exorbitant. Ferdinand and Isabel introduced some reforms in this area, ordering innkeepers to post signs stating current prices and the tips due to servants.

The Spaniards were somewhat spartan in their tastes, including their taste in food. Princess Juana's husband, Philip I, came from the Low Countries. When he introduced the long and elaborate dinners and drinking habits of the north to the Spanish court, many witnesses were shocked and frowned on such excesses. Francisco Villalobos, Ferdinand's personal physician, was concerned for people's health and wrote, "For myself, I prefer a pot full of garlic seasoned with olive oil, and cabbages that issue from the pot exhaling savory vapors, and laborer's bread that fills one's whole mouth and not some hollow stuff made only to please the palate." Probably, most Spaniards of the time would have agreed with him.

Festivals and Fiestas

During the time of Isabel and Ferdinand, Spaniards enjoyed many fiestas—celebrations that marked Christian holy days, saint's days, and seasonal changes. Each town and village had its own distinctive festivals, organized by brotherhoods called Cofradias. Many of these festivals are still celebrated today. Some were a curious blend of ancient pagan practices and Christian beliefs.

Everywhere in Spain, the Christmas season was the occasion for elaborate Nativity plays, which often included real shepherds and live sheep. In the village of Lesaca, in the kingdom of Navarre in northern Spain, the people celebrated by remembering the story of the charcoal burner. He was the person who came down from the mountains to tell the people the good news of Christ's birth. In the fiesta celebrating this event, a villager would be carried shoulder-high through the town on Christmas Eve.

One of the most exciting times of year was the period just before Lent. A carnival atmosphere would take hold just before the season of repentance. Authorities, such as the mayor of a town, would be mocked by children, and streets would be filled with revelers wearing huge masks and dancing to music. Freaks, fools, monsters, devils—all kinds of creatures—would be represented.

Mary Magdalene, a follower of Jesus, was a popular figure in

Spain. To honor her, the men of the mountain village of Anguiano developed a special tradition of dancing on stilts. During this July fiesta, the dancers wore long skirts that swirled out as they spun on their stilts, negotiating the steep streets almost in a trance. Their faith in the Magdalena promised them a safe journey to her shrine.

Chronicles of the thirteenth and fourteenth centuries mention the San Fermines that took place during October in Pamplona in Navarre. They were a combination of religious and commercial celebrations to promote trade, and included processions, dancing, and the display of livestock. A tradition developed in which dangerous bulls were let loose in the streets and daring young men risked their lives to race ahead of them, hoping to reach the bullring (where a bullfight would take place) alive. In Spain, bulls were (and still are) often at the heart of many festivals, perhaps because in pagan times, they were sacrificed to various gods. They also represent the Spanish ideals of courage and daring.

The fall was a quieter period in Spain, and festivals often reflected the need to prepare for the coming winter. Thus many fiestas featured the slaughter of animals for meat and the end of the harvest season. Feasts included traditional foods, such as *roscos* (cookies), *panelles* (sweet rolls), *tostones* (codfish), and roasted chestnuts, known as *magostos*.

All over Spain, at various times of the year, people reenacted the defeat of the Moors in annual festivals. Riding on horseback or

Bullfights attracted thousands of spectators. Early Iberians used to jump over the horns of a bull for sport. This developed into the art of the bullfighter, or toreador. Originally, toreadors fought on horseback. Later, they became even more daring and fought on foot.

on mules, Spaniards representing Christians and Moors would engage in mock battles. Of course, the followers of the Cross always triumphed, while the "Moors" were always banished.

The Spaniar

PART THREE

The ballads of El Cid, the eleventh-century Castilian warrior who battled the Moors, inspired artists down through time. In this nineteenth-century painting, Alfonso VI, king of Castile, swears on a Bible that he has not murdered El Cid's brother.

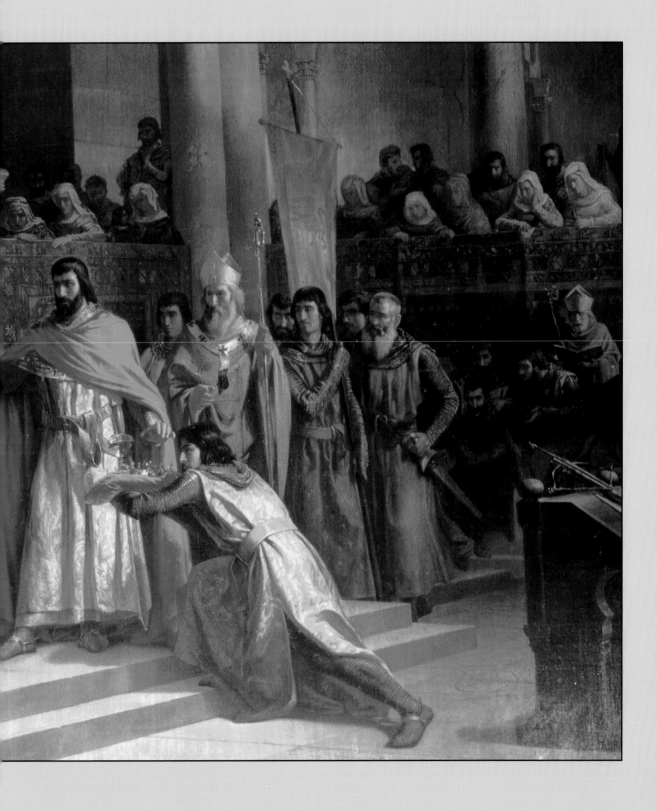

Ferdinand and Isabel were often apart, yet they stayed closely in touch via couriers. His letters to her are sometimes teasing and playful, revealing an intimacy rarely seen by the outside world. This one was written on May 16, 1475:

> *Although messengers come and go between us, you do not*
> *write to me, not for lack of paper and not for not knowing*
> *how to write but for insufficient love and haughtiness,*
> *and because you are in Toledo and I in the provinces . . .*
> *but some day we shall return to our first love. . . . If you*
> *do not want me to kill myself, you should write and tell*
> *me how you are.*

A very different Ferdinand is revealed in this letter, which was sent along with Columbus on his second voyage in 1493 and was

This ornate dish was made for Ferdinand and Isabel in 1496.

to be conveyed to the Taino/Arawak Indians of Haiti. The message is unmistakable: as long as the Indians obey Spanish authority, they will be treated well. If not, theirs will be a terrible fate:

You owe compliance as a duty to the King and we in his name will receive you with love and charity, respecting your freedom and that of your wives and sons and your rights of possession . . . in exchange for which Their Highnesses bestow many privileges and exemptions upon you. Should you fail to comply, or delay maliciously in so doing, we assure you that with the help of God we shall use force against you, declaring war upon you from all sides and with all possible means, and we shall bind you to the yoke of the Church and of Their Highnesses; we shall seize and enslave your persons, wives and sons, sell you or dispose of you as the King sees fit; we shall seize your possessions and harm you as much as we can as disobedient and resisting vassals.

The Edict of Expulsion of the Jews was signed by Isabel and Ferdinand on March 31, 1492, and would go into effect on July 31. Isaac Abrabanel and Abraham Senior were Jewish tax collectors, well known to the court. They tried to intercede on behalf of the Jews, and gained an audience with Isabel and Ferdinand. Later, Abrabanel recalled:

> *I pleaded with the king many times. I supplicated him thus: "Save, O king. Why do thus to thy servants? Lay upon us every tribute and ransom, gold and silver, and everything that the Children of Israel possess, they shall willingly give to their father. . . ." [But] like an adder which stoppeth its ears, he remained deaf to our appeals. The queen, also, was standing by his side, but she would not listen to our plea.*

The edict permitted Jews to "barter, alienate, and dispose of all their movable and immovable property, freely and at will . . . to

Abrabanel and Senior offered the monarchs thirty thousand ducats in an attempt to buy their freedom. At first, Ferdinand was tempted, but Torquemada entered, placing a crucifix on the table, and cried, "Judas sold Christ for thirty pieces of silver! You would sell Him for thirty thousand ducats. Here He is—take Him and sell Him." This act is said to have persuaded the monarchs to issue the edict expelling the Jews.

export their wealth and property, by sea or land, from our said kingdoms and dominions . . . provided they do not take away gold, silver, [or] money." But this was hardly realistic. In Aragon, Ferdinand confiscated Jewish real estate as security for Jewish "revenues" owed the Crown. In some towns, local authorities barred Jews from leaving their neighborhoods to seek buyers for their homes; in others, Jews could only ask the lowest possible prices. Landlords demanded three months' rent in advance and debtors refused to pay. In desperation, as the deadline grew near, Jews would exchange an orchard or a vineyard for a donkey, or give away their homes for a horse. The highways became choked with refugees who were often stoned, beaten, and robbed. Andrés Bernáldez, a priest, observed these events:

They went out from the lands of their birth, boys and adults, old men and children, on foot, and riding on donkeys and other beasts and in wagons. . . . They went by the roads and fields with much labor and ill-fortune, some collapsing, others getting up, some dying, others giving birth, others falling ill, so that there was no Christian who was not sorry for them. . . . The rabbis were encouraging them and making the women and boys sing and beat drums and tambourines, to enliven the people. And so they went out of Castile.

The centuries-long fusion of Christian, Jewish, and Muslim thought in Spain gave rise to a large body of literature that dealt with spiritual and mystical matters. The relationship of human beings to God was the main theme. Among the great writers of the day was Teresa of Ávila (1515–1582). She was a nun who worked to reform the order to which she belonged, and was later deemed a saint. From her pen flowed many books. The most important of them was *The Interior Castle*, published in 1577. Here is her introduction:

> *Consider your soul as a castle made out of a single*
> *diamond or of a transparent crystal, in which are many*

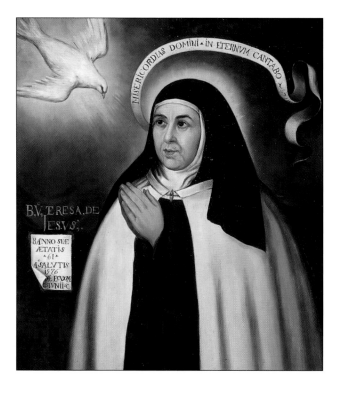

Teresa of Ávila was a gifted organizer as well as a mystic of extraordinary spiritual depth. When Protestantism gained ground elsewhere in Europe, she strengthened the forces that reformed the Roman Catholic Church from within.

rooms, just as in Heaven there are many mansions. . . .
Some of them are above, others below, others on both
sides; and in the midst, in the centre of them all, is the
chiefest of them where many things most secret pass
between God and the soul.

Almost everyone in fifteenth-century Spain would have been familiar with the heroic epic of El Cid, the great Castilian warrior who fought tirelessly against the Moors during the eleventh century. In fact, the many poems and ballads about El Cid, whose authors are unknown, are fictionalized accounts of the life of Rodrigo Díaz de Vivar (1043–1099), who was a vassal of King Alfonso VI of Castile. He was a distinguished knight, but eventually ran afoul of Alfonso and was banished from the kingdom. Rodrigo became a kind of vagabond mercenary, and even served the Muslim king of Zaragoza and other Muslim rulers. In the poems, however, Rodrigo—known as El Cid Campeador, or the Lord Champion—is portrayed as a brave, loyal servant of the king who is exiled because his enemies turn the king against him. El Cid continues to send Alfonso the spoils of his various conquests until he is returned to the king's favor. His life is one of honor, fidelity, humility, and duty—all the ideals that were typical of Spain at the time, and that persisted for centuries to come. The following stanzas describe the banishment of El Cid from Castile and the group of knights who gathered around him:

He turned and looked upon them and he wept very sore
As he saw the yawning gateway and the hasps wrenched off the door
And the pegs whereon no mantle nor coat . . . there hung
There perched no molting goshawk, and . . . no falcon swung.
My lord the Cid sighed deeply, such grief was in his heart,
And he spoke well and wisely: "Oh Thou in Heaven that art
Our Father and Our Master, now I give thanks to Thee.
Of their wickedness my foemen have done this thing to me. . . ."
A mighty feast they had prepared for the Great Campeador,
The bells within San Pedro they clamor and they peal.
That my lord the Cid is banished men cry throughout Castile.
And some have left their houses, from their lands some fled away.
Of knights an hundred and fifteen were seen upon that day,
By the bridge across the Arlanzon together they came o'er.
One and all were they calling on the Cid Campeador. . . .
My lord the Cid was merry that so great his commons grew,
And they that were come to him they all were merry too.
Six days of grace are over, and there are left but three,
Three and no more. The Cid was warned on his guard to be,
For the King said, if thereafter he should find him in the land,
Then neither gold nor silver should redeem him from his hand.
And now the day was over and night began to fall
His cavaliers unto him he summoned one and all:
"Hearken my noble gentlemen. And grieve not in your care.
Few goods are mine, yet I desire that each should have his share.
As good men ought, be prudent. When the cocks crow at day,
See that the steeds are saddled, nor tarry nor delay."

Although the Moors were gradually conquered, their culture remained very much alive in Spain. Much of their poetry survived the fall of Granada and was preserved by the Spaniards themselves in the Spanish language. While the texts remain, the authors are often unknown. Most of the poems deal with love, and many have an appealing sense of humor:

The Inconsistent

When I sent you my melons, you cried out with scorn,
They ought to be heavy and wrinkled and yellow;
When I offered myself, whom those graces adorn,
You flouted, and called me an ugly old fellow.

Many of the Moorish poems were actually ballads, or songs, written to be sung to the accompaniment of guitar and lute:

Zara's Earrings

"My earrings! My earrings! They've dropped into the well,
And what to say to Muca, I cannot, cannot tell."
Twas thus, Granada's fountain by, spoke Albuharez' daughter.

"The well is deep, far down they lie, beneath the cold blue water—
To me did Muca give them, when he spake his sad farewell,
And what to say when he comes back, alas! I cannot tell.

"My earrings! My earrings! They were pearls in silver set,
That when my Moor was far away, I ne'er should him forget,
That I ne'er to other tongue should list, nor smile on other's tale,
But remember he my lips had kissed, pure as those earrings pale—
When he comes back, and hears that I have dropped them in the well,

Oh, what will Muca think of me, I cannot, cannot tell.

"He'll think when I to market went, I loitered by the way;
He'll think a willing ear I lent to all the lads might say;
He'll think some other lover's hand, among my tresses noosed,
From the ears where he had placed them, my rings of pearl unloosed;
He'll think, when I was sporting so beside this marble well,
My pearls fell in—and what to say, alas! I cannot tell.

"I'll tell the truth to Muca, and I hope he will believe—
That I thought of him at morning, and thought of him at eve;
That, musing on my lover, when down the sun was gone,
His earrings in my hand I held, by the fountain all alone;
And that my mind was o'er the sea, when from my hand they fell,
And that deep his love lies in my heart, as they lie in the well."

During Isabel and Ferdinand's day, the notion of "chivalrous love" still inspired people. Men were moved by the same ideals of honor and glory that applied to the battlefield, and a knight would give his life in the service of these ideals and in order to win his lady's love. Hernando del Pulgar, the court chronicler for the Catholic Sovereigns, wrote that "the gentlemen tell them [women] that they are goddesses and that, for them, there are no other deities on heaven or earth; and that, if their ladies died, they would wish to be, not with God, but where their ladies were."

To fall in love was seen as a cruel trick of fate, and the poor lover was almost always condemned to suffering. The ladies were deemed infinitely superior to men: whatever they wished was granted; their command was the lover's law. Next to virtue, beauty was revered above all. Marriage was not necessarily the goal in these affairs of the heart. It was simply the adoration of a woman from afar:

> On whom shall I bestow my amorous verses—
> All gentle love with virtue entwined—
> If not on you, dear lady: yes, on you! . . .
> Receive them gently, if they so deserve;
> If not, receive them as you must. And if
> they overmuch do weep, be not annoyed
> By their fresh-flowing tears.

Glossary

anti-Semitism: Hatred of Jewish people and their faith, Judaism.

auto-da-fé: The burning of a heretic.

bureaucracy: An administration with many rules and regulations, run by many officers.

catalyst: Something that brings about change.

Celts: Ancient peoples of Western Europe whose descendants today include the Scottish, Irish, and Welsh, as well as the people of Galicia, an area in northern Spain.

conquistador: A Spanish soldier.

converso: A Jew who converted to Christianity.

Cortes: The legislative assembly of Spain.

heretic: A Christian whose opinions or practices go against the teachings of the church.

Iberians: The original inhabitants of the Iberian Peninsula.

Inquisition: The Roman Catholic court set up to root out heretics.

Maundy Thursday: The Thursday before Easter, commemorating Jesus' institution of Holy Communion.

pagan: Someone who is not Christian, Jewish, or Muslim.

regent: Someone who governs a kingdom during the period when the rightful ruler is too young, or unable, to take command.

Visigoths: Germanic tribes who entered Roman territories at the end of the fourth century and later established a kingdom in Spain.

For Further Reading

Barber, Richard. *The Reign of Chivalry*. New York: St. Martin's, 1980.

Brenner, Barbara. *If You Were There in 1492*. New York: Bradbury Press, 1991.

Fuson, Robert H. *The Log of Christopher Columbus*. Camden, ME: International Marine, 1987.

Haskins, James. *Religions*. New York: Lippincott, 1973.

McKendrick, Melveena. *The Horizon Concise History of Spain*. New York: American Heritage, 1972.

Powell, Anton. *The Rise of Islam*. New York: Warwick, 1980.

Stewart, Gail B. *Life during the Spanish Inquisition*. San Diego: Lucent Books, 1998.

ON-LINE INFORMATION*

http://www.fordham.edu/halsall/
An excellent place to find original texts as well as essays and commentary from academic authorities, with plenty of links to related websites for all ages.

http://www.win.tue.nl/cs/fm/engels/discovery
Provides excellent biographies of individuals as well as good background information on the era.

http://www.clark.net/pub/jumpsam/fiestas
Very informative on all of Spain's festivals, with pictures and historical as well as current information.

*Websites change from time to time. For additional on-line information, check with the media specialist at your local library. You can do your own research by typing in keywords such as Medieval Spain, Catholic Monarchs, Isabel of Spain, Iberian Peninsula, or Age of Exploration.

Bibliography

Aries, Philippe. *Centuries of Childhood: A Social History of Family Life.* Translated by Robert Baldick. New York: Knopf, 1962.

Brenner, Barbara. *If You Were There in 1492.* New York: Bradbury Press, 1991.

Crow, John. *Spain: The Root and the Flower.* Berkeley: University of California Press, 1985.

Davies, R. Trevor. *The Golden Century of Spain, 1501–1621.* London: Macmillan & Co., 1954.

Ford, J. D. M. *Main Currents of Spanish Literature.* New York: Henry Holt, 1919.

Giardini, Cesare. *The Life & Times of Columbus.* Translated by Frances Lanza. Curtis Internationale, 1967.

Green, Otis H. *Spain and the Western Tradition.* Vol. 1. Madison: University of Wisconsin Press, 1963.

Horne, Charles F. *The Sacred Books and Early Literature of the East.* Vol. 6, *Medieval Arabia.* New York: Parke, Austin & Lipscomb, 1917.

Kamen, Henry. *The Spanish Inquisition—A Historical Revision.* New Haven: Yale University Press, 1999.

Liss, Peggy K. *Isabel the Queen: Life and Times.* New York: Oxford University Press, 1992.

Mariejol, Jean Hippolyte. *The Spain of Ferdinand and Isabella.* Translated and edited by Benjamin Keen. New Brunswick: Rutgers University Press, 1961.

Merriman, R. B. *The Spanish Empire.* Vol. 2. New York: n.p., 1934.

Pierson, Peter. *The History of Spain.* Westport, CT: Greenwood Press, 1999.

Plunket, Ierne L. *Isabel of Castile and the Making of the Spanish Nation 1451–1504*. New York: G. P. Putnam's Sons, 1915.

Prescott, William H. *Histories: The Rise and Decline of the Spanish Empire*. New York: Viking Press, 1963.

Rose, R. Seldon, and Leonard Bacon, trans. *The Lay of the Cid*. Berkeley: University of California Press, 1919.

Sachar, Howard M. *Farewell España*. New York: Vintage Books, 1994.

Virgoe, Roger, ed. *Private Life in the Fifteenth Century: Illustrated Letters of the Paston Family*. London: Weidenfield & Nicolson UK, 1989.

Notes

p. 18 "She was able": Plunket, *Isabel of Castile and the Making of the Spanish Nation*, p. 328.

p. 22 "he had so singular a grace": Liss, *Isabel the Queen*, p. 75.

p. 24 "very gallant": Plunket, *Isabel of Castile and the Making of the Spanish Nation*, p. 73.

p. 25 Notes on population estimates: Merriman, *Spanish Empire*, vol. 2, p. 93.

p. 29 "in these kingdoms": Kamen, *The Spanish Inquisition in the Sixteenth and Seventeenth Centuries*, p. 84.

p. 40 "Such great grief": Liss, *Isabel the Queen*, p. 332.

p. 40 "she was the best": Liss, *Isabel the Queen*, p. 353.

p. 64 "Although messengers": Liss, *Isabel the Queen*, p. 112.

p. 66 "I pleaded with the king": Sachar, *Farewell España*, p. 70.

p. 66 "Judas sold Christ": *The Catholic Encyclopedia*, Vol. 14; Online Edition 1999; www.newadvent.org/cathen/147783a.htm

p. 67 "They went out": Sachar, *Farewell España*, p.73.

p. 68 "Consider your soul": Davies, *The Golden Century of Spain*, p. 292.

p. 70 "He turned and looked": Rose and Bacon, *The Lay of the Cid*, p. 58.

p. 71 "The Inconsistent": Horne, *The Sacred Books and Early Literature of the East*, p. 249.

p. 71 "Zara's Earrings": Horne, *The Sacred Books and Early Literature of the East*, p. 254.

p. 73 "On whom": Green, *Spain and the Western Tradition*, p. 129.

Index

Page numbers for illustrations are in boldface.